Speak to Strangers

Gemma Seltzer is a London-based writer and literary blogger. She is interested in charting her creative responses to people and places through interactive web-based projects. Her fiction has been published in *.Cent* magazine and as part of an exhibition catalogue commissioned by The Photographers' Gallery and ArtSway. She spoke at the 2009 Venice Biennale about the relationship between contemporary art and text. Gemma is the author of *Look up at the Sky,* an online activity exploring the peace and the pauses in the city.

Speak to Strangers
Gemma Seltzer

Penned in the Margins

LONDON

PUBLISHED BY PENNED IN THE MARGINS
53 Arcadia Court, 45 Old Castle Street, London E1 7NY
www.pennedinthemargins.co.uk

First published 2011

Printed in the United Kingdom by MPG Biddles Ltd.

ISBN
978-0-9565467-9-1

FT
Pbk

ACKNOWLEDGEMENTS

Thank you to my one hundred strangers for unwittingly offering me creative fodder. I am also very grateful to my parents, Lynne and Gerry Seltzer, for their encouragement and joyfulness; to my sister Carly Seltzer for laughing at the phrase 'flaccid earlobes' and to Craig Osborne for reading every one of the stories. Thanks to the colleagues and friends who offered support of magnificent proportions, particularly Rachel Cherry, Mark Hopkinson, Miriam Lessar, Cecilia Magill, Emily Oliver and Amy Racs.

Reema Fadda, Peter Law, Kim Patrick and Nikesh Shukla provided invaluable literary and digital wisdom - thank you! For their kindness and distractions, I'd also like to thank Emily Bromfield, Laura Cattell, Kate Costello, Kristin Dasgupta, Lily Rose Davies, George Fox, Claire Haslam, Helli Mason, Katrina Naomi, Stephen Nash, AnneMarie Neligan, Jo Philips with .Cent magazine, and Silvi Subba. Thanks are due to my editor Tom Chivers, for wondering how the blog might look as a book. Most of all, thank you to the lovely Mathew Hanratty for offering flowers, and much else besides.

I've freely borrowed from writers and artists I admire and people I know. As David Shields advocates, reality cannot be copyrighted, but I thank them all here for their words and ideas.

For MH; and yet, and yet.

Speak to Strangers

Day 1

My mind was elsewhere when you asked me about my default printer. I don't have the right one. I have the wrong one. I wanted to know why, but you couldn't explain. Heads turned, also needing an answer. How can something change overnight? We need routine here. A solution would come, you promised us. I saw how you described my needs on your clipboard, both names spelt incorrectly and a dash leading to a series of numbers. This is how you represent my needs. I want to throw off my cardigan and the cold air to fall on my skin.

Day 2

Too much noise and a sadness that followed you room to room. You liked the balcony, but wouldn't go outside. You wanted a series of rails along the walls. Body in slumped heaps; your eyes darted about, asking questions that sounded like pleas. Like me, want me, take me. A certain type of direct enquiry repels, makes me recoil, but you wouldn't know. You aimed, drew back and shot. As it hit, venom rose. It was like tasting something not consumed since childhood. It brought anxiety with it, as much as anger. I closed the door behind as you left.

Day 3

I like a man waiting for me. I like to be late, just a little, to add a bit more suspence to the encounter. Your glasses were angled, your teeth aligned. And that emphatic way you spoke with both hands as you explained what it was you wanted from me then. I filled in my details, careful not to smudge, whilst you read your papers, fiddled with your collar. Around us, glasses clinked, a large television screen showed heavy-set rugby players grappling with each other's bodies and the jukebox played songs by Kylie Minogue. You didn't check your watch once.

Day 4

Where were you looking? Not at me, or at them, but into the distance, beyond the street where we all stood. Your height, that might have been it, or perhaps your recent good fortune, made you distant. You spoke of shopping, holidays and your partner's recent success. There was gossip. I think we all laughed; you smiled. You wore a gold chain around your neck and that's all I could see. I pointed towards the heath; you only stared at my hairline. Carrying two bags in each hand, your arm muscles and teeth swallowed the strain. Your conversational skills suffered.

Day 5

From a distance, your hands look perfect. Tapered fingers that lead to cuticles of white moons, nails of pearls. A silver ring looping over your middle finger. I listen as you tell me I'm a Reflector with Activist instincts. There's nodding; apparently it's true. I'm a known entity and I admire your insights. There's no clock in the room. We tell the time through conversations ending. Later I observe that it's fake; the nails are stuck on. I see the glue, the orange streak along your forearm. Your smile is permanent. I wonder what it is that makes you happy.

Day 6

Your hair falls in the same way mine does, over one shoulder, uneven ends trailing to your chest. You're roughly a head taller than me but that might be your shoes. A name like yours is unnatural shortened but still, you have chosen this label that trips me up. It's too immediately familiar. You speak about a new opportunity, not with wistfulness but restlessness. It will tie you down and you want absolute freedom. In you, there is a bright glowing place. I'd like to see you stand upright, holding a cigarette between angled fingers, hair piled on your head.

Day 7

It's your job, so you shouldn't be ashamed. You seem too delicate for the work you've chosen. Do you also step back when asked a question in the operating theatre? Do you shy away from cleaning the wound, say it's not something you could manage? Do you ask for air, when you really want escape? It seems significant that you work through the night and also peer into the cupboard rather than open it. And yet, I judge too much. You're perfectly competent, no doubt. Conversations are easier when we speak of what we do, rather than what we want.

Day 8

Latte, espresso, cappuccino. Helpfulness is next to godliness. Friendliness is akin to kindness. Cleanliness and white walls are much like peace. I came here to be alone with strangers and to type. You catch my eye, bring me things, realign the curtains and give me two passes when I ask for just one. You're younger than me, have dark eyes. At every other table, a woman holds her baby. The husbands wear black-rimmed glasses and have booming voices. You talk to them all. Here, I won't ask for coffee because I'm too aware of my fertility levels. Redbush, peppermint, camomile.

Day 9

There is nothing notable about you until I see how immense your eyes are behind your glasses. I tell you a funny story to see if it really is funny. And sure enough, you laugh. I concentrate on how you structure your response, the anecdote you choose in reply, so I can remember it later. It's a way to lessen the impact of the facts. Through the repetition of these words, I can get used to the situation. As I listen to our exchange, I think, Yes, this is something I can say; this is something I can live through.

Day 10

There's music in my ears but I can still hear the sound my shoes make on the pavement, clashing against the ground like a ticking clock. My mouth has been sealed shut since I woke and no one has looked me in the eye. Our exchange is slight. I take my fruit and offer you the exact change in an open palm. You don't react, only pick the money with fingerless gloves. I want to not give you anything, not share myself. I want you to not hear my voice. I can't think about anything if I have to talk.

Day 11

You are watching a portable television as you serve me. There are several drums and wind instruments playing music and you are engrossed. I take my time selecting the items I want. I pick things up, examine, think, then put them down again, listening and hiding from the rain. You are out of place in Exmouth Market. You sell what people actually want. I need Hula Hoops. I have chosen a flavour I usually avoid. Can I tell you this? No. I arrange my choices in the shape of a smiley face. I'm ready. You don't even glance at me.

Day 12

You had a panicked query. How do I get to Old Street? And because I knew,
I felt a sense of inrush, an internal torrent of happiness. You were leaning
over the passenger seat; it looked painful, calling to me through the open
window. I threw my arm to the right: It's this way! I gave excited directions,
showing how to get onto Farringdon Road and curving my hand round to
demonstrate where you might turn. You relaxed on hearing my confident
comments and I actually clapped when you said thank you, knowing that I
had done well that day.

Day 13

You're not an attention seeker; you just wanted to know if we liked the cakes. We don't answer you until you are out of earshot. I think we are unlikely to be friends. You are not someone who drives to work and has a designated parking space. You have an apron and crumbs on your fingers. You spill my drink and mop it up with a dirty cloth and I talk over your apology because I'm not in the mood for this. I look at the couple on the next table: nine macaroons, a bottle of wine and holding hands.

Day 14

The music is louder than your voice and you keep your jacket on all night. As we speak, sweat trails along your temples and you dab your neck with a tissue. Your shirt underneath is ornate like a curtain. Share the pattern. Why be shy of perspiring? It's the way of the dance floor. Talking to you makes me want to pick my own pockets, pour whisky and lemonade down my throat and throw ice cubes at the grimy men in the DJ booth. If you get any closer, I'll just move aside so you can stand where I stood.

Day 15

I quickly see that asking you for directions is the wrong choice. It is raining and I am late and you turn your body as you turn the map in your hands. You tell me I'm not far. Your beagle has the look of an impatient child, sniffing, barking, pecking at my feet. Something about Golders Hill Park makes you happy. You say the words over and over, using your teeth to smile, as though the path I need to take will become clearer with each mention. I ask about gold. You flick your wrist from me to the path.

Day 16

It was not the first time I'd been, but was the first time you were there. You had plastic gloves and you and your companion both recommended the falafel wraps. Ignoring the cheese and tomato garnish, I distracted you with questions about the refurbishment. You were proud, you had high expectations. You did not know where the previous owners went. You bought the place and painted it white. Being in your café was like standing high on a cliff top and gazing over the edge. We were surrounded by the bloated silence below, kept away by only a thin brink.

Day 17

Interrupting your conversation, I confuse you both. A life-size doll's house, Ikea is strangely intimate. I sit on the sofa, examining a ladle and admiring the Alvine Räffla cushion cover design, whilst you two joke about the night ahead and which of you has on better earrings. I trip over my own words. If I'd had a pot of tea, I'd have offered you a cupful, but instead I imagine I am in your home and that your 'Can I Help You?' badges mean more than suggesting furnishing advice. I think I should have chosen the red, not the paisley.

Day 18

All the nice men grow moustaches in November, even if they find it exposing in surprising ways. I say, Do it, when you ask if you should tick my name off the list. You say, Do what? and I say, Do Do. It's a good thing your hair is dark. I say, I'm going to meet someone downstairs, and you say, That's fine, but don't forget to come back. I say, I won't and then I do, instead talking to my friend about books, jobs, hair, tissues. When I finally return later you remember me and say, Go straight in.

Day 19

This is the first time I've not wanted to speak to a stranger. I'm tired of trying. I see the puffed ruffled sleeves on your shirt and how the elastic trim is digging into your forearms. You pull a pint, you announce it with a raised eyebrow. I have nothing more to report. You take my money, you return my change. I've done this too many times now. I request the time, just to say something. You glance at your watch and tell me. And the man next to me orders shandy and asks me if I think it's late.

Day 20

I've started clocking strangers before I notice friends. I tell you about this project, then feel regret. It's hard to speak to someone if they think they could have any face and be anyone. You're livelier than the rest of us and tell a better story. We're an even number and we refer to each other in abbreviations. I explain what I do. I hear the warning in my own words. And so I will write of you like this and of the monkey on a string, slanting pencils of light, the cold evening, specks of dust in the air.

Day 21

I take my place at the till and you tell me how much you're looking forward to X Factor. The twins are very bad and you laugh when you see them. They are bad, you say, very bad. Their haircuts! Your name is Ivy. I hear about the judges, bad too, as I pack my shopping and then say I don't own a television. This is important information for you. What do I do without it? Books, radio and cups of tea. You look at my organic oakcakes, frown, and then tell me I could still catch the show online.

Day 22

I run in the rain, through the heath, along a private road, to the park. The donkeys wave. Two owls peer out. You have a toy airplane in your hand and make it sweep through the air. You lift it up to show the others, making it fly over their heads. Look! you say. Magic. I speak to you and your three little brothers who sit on their bikes, in height order, and stare at me as I jog pass. You tell me to look for the deer. My day takes on a new shape, loses some of its thorniness.

Day 23

Our voices sound similar, our natural register alike. I shift mine to a whispering tone, you raise yours as you tell me about paying excessively for your parking. You play the part of an angry customer and I am a civilised and reasonable manager. I tug at a loose thread on my skirt and watch as it escapes from tiny holes on the hem. Afterwards, I conclude the exchange and I walk you to the door. I think I stand too close. When I see you in Benetton later that day, you avoid me, playing another part. Shopper. Actress. Stranger.

Day 24

The door jangles like Christmas. You are engrossed in a large-print wordsearch. You have an entire puzzle book. I remember sitting with my grandma, finding the letters together, using a red pen. You wear a t-shirt, glasses slipping down your nose. Fairylights are sellotaped around the counter. I present my jacket in a damp lump; you say it's nothing a dry clean won't sort out. And you say confidence, enthusiasm and a smile will guarantee success. What I like best about you is your flashy jewellery and that you want to speak to me as much as I to you.

Day 25

I trip over your chair, an embarrassing entrance, but it makes for an immediate introduction. We shake hands. You're pleased to meet me. You describe things as wonderful or heartbreaking. Under the first agenda point, I volunteer a project idea. Pens scribble and I write it down myself, to remember, to join in. You touch the collar of your leather jacket and speak of women in prisons. The air is full of tentative, eager exchanges, with something in it sad and regretful. I drink a peppermint tea. We all do. This speaks volumes about the type of people we are.

Day 26

You clutch your health food shop bag and discuss the deterioration of modern living, how we're all Blair's puppets and that the teenager in a red dress, laughing at her book, is the only one who understands. It is my only opportunity today so I make the most of it, to the disgust of the carriage. I ask you to repeat yourself, Did you say we're all going to die? You mumble a response, and then yelp: You can't hear me! No one hears me! I do, but seeing the first fury of your despair I decide to turn away.

Day 27

The maternal way of you the shrug of your shoulders. Can I describe a time I used advocacy skills not really can you? Is your hair red is it the light what else can I think about what else have I thought about since I knew I had to do this? You nod when I talk I pause to see if you keep nodding you do so I think it's not really what I am saying but that I am talking and filling the silence with something. Am I right for this I think you might know or you will.

Day 28

I tried to explain why I used so much energy to push the door open, but you weren't interested. You see, I have waited outside here before, not realising the door was just stiff. I was witness to sparkly young ladies necking drinks and watching a bride to be unwrap presents. The way a woman laughs can give an insightful notion of what she's like in other areas: shrieking, cooing, some eye rolling or groaning. I thought it was just jammed, until you called, 'It's occupied'. You weren't keen to hear my story, leaving the cubicle in such a fatal, furious manner.

Day 29

You walk into the shop, shaved head, downturned mouth and ask for Chanukah candles. The small ones are cheap and colourful but last only a couple of hours, so the thick, plaited choice suits. You need to concentrate; you lean your umbrella against the shelves. As you decide, I see you twist the skin on your wrist as far as it will go, maybe to make sure you do still have skin, that it reacts when touched and that it responds to pressure. When you release your grip, a scarlet depression remains, and you seem elated. Today, it's raining again.

Day 30

You remind me of PJ Harvey: eyeshadow in green streaks and the dark, vague look of you. You have a clipboard; you introduce us to someone and point to the canapés. The way you do this is efficient and swift. And then you're gone. There are three judges, two speeches and one award. I have a glass of wine and I know I'll have more. Things happen, or they don't happen. Later, city sunset over you, you are bleary and searching for name badges. I think about how we really are all pretending to know what we say we know.

Day 31

I play back everything that has happened today and this might be the most significant moment. Life roars in front sometimes, reminding you, or me, that it's there. Currently, my world is seen through Amy Hempel coloured glasses so though I can't hear your whisper voice and you forget my drink order twice, when I realise you find it hard to look directly at customers, I see you brighter than before, more damaged and anxious. Under the arch of white walls and Christmas menus that face the door, you put black pepper on my pizza in the most profound way.

Day 32

We're not sure this counts because I actually need to speak to strangers in meetings, but it's my encounter for the day so I will tell about it. You wear a beret and say it's because you are playing a part. You agree with most things, then afterwards you disagree. You have more opinions that I imagine you keep to yourself. Maybe we're all too young to know better. I wait for your response to each point, I want to be in your team. We live the noble life, making changes, feeling the sheer power of routine and choosing hats.

Day 33

I ask you about the closing time of the gallery and because I call it this rather than museum, collection, or exhibition, I hesitate before finishing my sentence. You don't know quite what I'm asking. You look up from your book, not with your head but with your eyelids. My big sister is small beside me and even though I talk to you, I'm really mocking her or me. Too much art gives her a headache, so we find our own entertainment: how I misjudge corners, her ugly twin fascination and taking identical steps up and down the spiral staircase.

Day 34

In South America, women weave fireflies in their hair. In London, two men stare at the tube map above my head, make a decision on their route, then realise they are travelling in the wrong direction. Between them – not literally – they have six teenagers who call them Dad or Dave or Uncle Michael. The girls own hair straighteners and friendship bands. A lone boy doesn't know what to say to them all. There's chanting and falling into seats. I help them follow the navy blue line to Russell Square. It's not far, I tell them. Change here, mind the gap.

Day 35

I suppose I'm saying, I'm here now and I wonder for how long. I don't know the answer. You look around, are slight and friendly. We like you, we all make each other laugh. Zac Efron is mentioned. I tug on the end of my hair. Flat viewings are so much like blind dates. You ask how we met and we're reluctant to say. It was summer, we were much younger. You touch the walls and I want your scarf and your hair. I find myself saying the same things to everyone. You are calmer than anyone I've ever met.

Day 36

I have bright fingernails and I only notice you because you are all in black. I'm a rainbow; you're not. I'm swinging my red bag, I'm tying my blue scarf, I've snagged my teal tights. Sophie Calle has been asking strangers to decode her romantic failings / flailings. In this crowded vocal room, everyone wonders how they would respond. You stand in front of the Writer. Her interpretation says, Beware all these women gathered together. You have a shirt that buttons to your neck. Already today, I've seen three people from my past. I want you to say something new.

Day 37

Both of you are drinking wine. The shop is dusty and lacy. I pick handkerchiefs out of a basket whilst you hear each other's opinions on Paul O'Grady. He should have his own prime time show. The jokes he tells! I lean on the counter and talk about my grandma's compact, how it smashed when I dropped it down an escalator. I'd forgotten this sadness. You show me a mirror decorated with thistles, once owned by another person's relative. Your friend rummages inside her handbag, desperately seeking something. I smile an attempt at a smile and arrow towards the door.

Day 38

My hair is still damp from the rain and I flick the tips towards a stranger. Where can we powder our noses? We ask you because it is necessary to transform ourselves with carefully placed kirby grips and shiny lips. You start to give directions but your voice fades because your eyes watch an elderly woman who has spilled red wine on her silk dress and has several people pawing unhelpfully at her dress with napkins. We hear her say, Thank you ever so much, laughing so her curls shake like chocolate shavings on a dessert. Follow her, you say.

Day 39

You speak of inconsequential things: petty cash, sandwiches and bank fees. I glance at the stall but am burdened by the pressures of time and the wretched weather. I pick up a teacup and your eyes dart towards me. You could have asked! I apologise and, as atonement, I begin to order other items I have touched. You slap my hand away. I think this: I browse and – if I buy or if I don't – my day is still crowned with purpose. The search is reason enough. For you, disdain for me is a culmination of all your failed sales.

Day 40

From the diner, we see a woman rip a parking notice from the windscreen and take photographs of her car. I ask you for water. There are three of you serving us, you merge into one person with short hair, ponytails and the beginnings of a beard. You are all friendly or young. Behind the glass, an oak tree has lost its leaves. Nature is outside of here. How can we change when we don't know where we were before? You offer ketchup and I pour it all over my burger, eat desperately, thinking of rotting apple cores, ruined crops.

Day 41

Like teenagers, we rub make up on our skin and ask naive questions about face cream. Tissue wrapped around your middle fingers, you sit her down, wipe her face and speak about the importance of cleansing. You dab something pink onto her cheeks and ask me if I prefer this colour, or that. I don't know and choose to wander instead. I buy products I definitely don't need and smell the entire range of celebrity perfumes on offer. Britney's is potent. Back at the counter, you demonstrate with many bottles and encourage me to think more carefully about my looks.

Day 42

I step outside and you move away, think again and return to where you were. You're on your mobile phone, you're prodding at the keys and then you tell me I'm only hurting myself by standing in the cold instead of in the pub. I tell you alcohol is evil and I only ever drink pure green tea. You say that you used to have accidents when you drank cider, but the part that hurt was never the part that got hurt. I recommend elderflower, I praise freshly squeezed lemonade. You say life is too short not to choose Guinness.

Day 43

I'm ready for a challenge. I'm at Spitalfields on a Sunday, one hour, two important items to find and a mulled wine appointment to keep. I touch everything at the handmade paper stall and try on short dresses. Wrapped in a Tibetan blanket, you have silk trimming across your chest and feathers decorating your fringe. I'm at home here. I try on hairbands and you readjust the beads for me. I tell you how long I've been looking for you and you laugh gloriously into your hands. Nearby, a dog as big as a pony barks, terrified at the crowd.

Day 44

We wash our hands all in a row. You glare at me and I know you are waiting to speak to me. You'd tried at the bar, but I didn't hear. What I also know is that in the bathroom, you narrow your eyes and say I shouldn't drink absinthe. I'm not alone, but you single me out to tell me why my complexion is flawed. Unpleasant and so much so, but maybe not everything needs to be a battle. I wonder if there are other people like us, sharing a moment like this, in a bar, in this city.

Day 45

I haven't slept, so the thoughts I'm having aren't quite right. I think of how I take myself to the edge of places, to look over and see. You are lively, Scottish and sitting on the corner of your chair. Of course, I'm late but this is funny, not problematic. The room is stuffy, the air rather soupy. You talk about the new protocol, how we will still comment on grant applications. The only questions I can think of are about your personal life: what makes you this way? Who tells you they love you? Is this what you want?

Day 46

Teenage girls use their handbags for cover as they run screeching through the streets. They splash through puddles together, with two of them holding hands. I step into the shop and fill a basket, just for fun, with everything that has aloe vera as an ingredient. Afterwards, I return each item to the wrong shelf, brush my teeth in the aisle and curl my hair by the pharmacy counter. You won't take my money until I find my Boots card. We could be here some time, I say. With your back against the door, you're before me like a shield.

Day 47

You are both informal and formal, or one of you is one and the other the other. Mercifully, you acknowledge the humour in this. I'm dressed for this interview, articulate and enthusiastic. Formal or informal tells me I look like her sister-in-law. You are mothers and have young children. It's snowing and I'm talking about audience engagement, but who will be coming to the gallery when the weather is like this? One of you has inky eyes and the look of a person anxious for the end of something, the process of asking people the same list of questions probably.

Day 48

Listening to carols on Classic FM leaves me feeling nostalgic for a childhood I never had. There are glowing trees in living rooms and - in pubs with steamed windows - men wear festive ties. It's this season and my state of mind is significant. It strikes me that twenty-seven years of Christmases can be reduced to a simple, descriptive chain of happy or painful events and people. The sweet shop is new I discover, as I pick up jelly beans, chocolate footballs and sugared almonds. I tell you they're all for me. No doubt, you've heard this said before.

Day 49

You make dresses for musical theatre and we are completely captivated. Your boyfriend disappears into the crowd as we ask about sewing, fabric, sweat, tutus and your thoughts on the updated designs for Les Mis. You have salt and pepper hair, and hold the lead for your dog all evening. I encourage you tell us about the time you dressed up in a corset; you do and then lament the size of your waist now. We grip our own bodies self-consciously. I could dive into your world and breaststroke my way somewhere else, head elevated above the current, mouth pinched.

Day 50

The metal hooks on the wall look like taps. I glance along the racks of necklaces and bracelets and imagine the hooks leaking, dripping from their joints, spilling out water that would eventually cover the floor, making a riverbed of the route to the train station. You're by my side, asking me if I need help. Yes, in so many ways but start with this woollen hat. Taking it from me, you jump – actually jump – and loop it back onto the clip. Then you draw your hands behind your back as if to get away without the moment touching you.

Day 51

You swear and thump the door. You're reading about Dunkirk and your eyes flick from the page, to me, to the flashing tunnel interior. I think you might not be the type to talk about your feelings. Your neck is thick and you blame London Underground, the Mayor, the government and lazy people. On my side of the carriage, a woman laughs at her newspaper, a baby cries and a flower of panic blooms inside of me but still I say what I need to. I tell you we're nearly there. It's fine, just a delay, is the book good?

Day 52

It's not the conversation we're having that keeps us talking, rather it's the place it takes us to. Which is why losing my hat again feels like losing a sense of reality. How easy I seem to mislay items of clothing. I return to the café and you have my beret hanging from a lampshade. You have red hair, a quiff and ask me if I was cold. I tell you I don't know, but then touch my icy ears, self-conscious. I breathe the air of things done differently, of how it might be to live without a covered head.

Day 53

I ask for tofu and you say this is possible. I want red bean cakes and this is feasible, too. I take my bento box and sit in a pink chair, admire the red heart-shaped table decorations. Should a café show its romantic aspirations so openly? I eat, see you laughing into your companion's shoulder. Your thoughts might be food-shaped. The pointed shoes you choose, your plans to own a gallery or fly to Iceland, all in the shape of vegetables. I see the thoughts as balloons, with you holding the strings as they float above your giggling, aspirational head.

Day 54

There's humming, clapping and singing. Your hair is brushed back, covered with a circular cloth. You try hard to pay attention, to hear the words we choose to greet you with. We're not asking you to carry a lot of rocks in your sleeves, just to open a little, to say something honest, to look closely and see us. When you're sad, you take a front row cinema seat. I think someone loves you boldly, wholly. A week, a month, a year, it's all good for you, I think. You smile, then wave ahead. There's someone else who desires you.

Day 55

You are whispering by the kitchen. I have never heard a person speak so softly. I think you are waiting for something and are scared it may not come. Holding a jar of parmesan, you touch the elbow of your fellow waiter. In contrast, there's cutlery and white plates, wine glasses and a coughing fit, someone hammering frantically, desperate to finish the shed, affix the trellis or whatever people do that makes so much noise. This music for the suburbs, this DIY as a percussion solo, this constant sound that hides voices, grabs my throat and assaults my peaceful mind.

Day 56

With your eyes on me, you say - Look, about the other night. Your throat, it might be dry. You're not sure you should bring this up. An easy life is talking about things, all sorts of things, rather than listening to the actual words. - We don't need to do this now, I reply. You: - I just couldn't do it. It didn't feel right. That's all. Me: - When I'm with you, I experience many different types of emptiness. Maybe none of this happens, or some of it, or hardly. I probably just ask for a slice of cake, that one, please.

Day 57

To call the legal department, I dial six numbers. You chirp when you answer. During our exchange, you are alternately friendly and distant like a child on a swing, back and forth, coming back. It has hands, your voice. It journeys to my forehead, strokes gently, slaps, strokes again. As I speak, I note how well you listen, so I catch this moment in my fist and when you tell me I need to fill in a form, I am ready to share truths. I say something about the nature of neediness, adoration and a heart that will not settle.

Day 58

Someone has fainted and you leap to help, when a woman stops you with a single finger. Her hair straightened to extremity, thick heavy locks that hang assertively. You try again but she uses two fingers this time to make sure you stay. Seeing this, you understand. It seems you hold out your arms for this dominance and then you take it. Putting it on, it's like a woollen blanket, for you to wrap around yourself. You look at her with such devoted submission. Your mind says, someone else will help. To your yielding, I may be the only witness.

Day 59

Brave people leap out of airplanes with only a slow-releasing parachute for company, scuba dive to the sound of their husky breath, perform emotion as art in public. I've done these things but when you say you have too, the words turn to heavy boots and you're stamping on my experiences. They become sodden leaves, pulverized to a pulp. You're a graphic designer and that makes me think you draw comics for a living. In contrast, I tell you I love the pamphlet you created, using terms like adore, admire and respect. I enthuse because it's all I can do.

Day 60

Because you must see the world from such a low angle, because your face is a smile and because I am full of wine, I start a conversation. You wear a woollen hat, dense red lipstick and grip your handbag. I suppose it's tough to be so small, I say. Affection and intrigue cram themselves in me, bring with them a racing mind and heart. Inside, I feel like a house slowly regaining power after a black out, the boiler purring to life, the lights hesitating then glowing, the radio shouting from a disaster zone. You say, It is rather.

Day 61

We're standing in the lift with you and your Irish husband, who apologises for touching you in public. You missed the evening showing of Billy Elliot and chose dinner, wine and facing each other in your seats instead. It is decided that we've all had pleasant evenings, that we like Chalk Farm, that it's late and that as there's a tube waiting on the platform, so we should run. Trapped in the closing doors until someone releases me, I think how blonde your hair is, how dark your skin, how white your stilettos and how different your name from his.

Day 62

When your wife died, you dug honeysuckle into the edges of your garden. A plant that grew rapidly, soon clambering across the entire fence, strangling your Hibiscus syriacus. It sprouted pale flowers, filling the air with sweetness. How deceptive, the natural world; beautiful yet so fierce, you say. I imagine you at your kitchen window, looking out and thinking, There is only Nature, as there is only Now. Like a kick in the chest. Now. The word itself is inadequate. Keep moving, tidy, eat, see, while the world around you dies, lives and dies again. You hand me my change.

Day 63

An arm swipes my face, leaning to take our empties. A series of games machines flash nearby. You complain under your breath. Later, at the bar, you despise my drinks orders, hate that I also want crisps. This has become a familiar feeling. This dull sensation of inevitability, the sheer power of sameness, that nothing ever changes, that pubs are pubs are pubs, would always be pubs. In one corner, men with loosened ties share loud conversations. Thick-necked rugby players grope and spit at each other on the television screen. Somewhere nearby, someone is humming a song by The Smiths.

Day 64

The man behind the counter brandishes a bouquet of cutlery. I'll have that one, you say, pointing and fluttering eyelashes, thick mascara clapping together in a suggestive round of applause. That one, then. You reach out for one and he draws them away. Come on! you say, really meaning, don't stop, don't stop. It's very humorous for you both. Or it is, until I grab a fork and jam it into my unhurried sandwich, waiting to be paid for. They are astonished. They've never seen such behaviour! In an adult, too! Sorry, I say, and I do slightly mean it.

Day 65

Embarrassingly, I have to ask what Bubble and Squeak is. So many English traditions seem to have rushed passed me, ungraspable, like ploughed fields and neat back gardens from a smudged train window. You are Russian and have hair backcombed at odd angles. There is lipstick gathered in the corner of your mouth and, as you suggest other menu options, I realise I can't move on from my default position of younger child. I'm stuck here, at this age, hearing someone tell me what to eat and nodding, wanting to please, yet – as always – never quite sure what I want.

Day 66

I'm on the periphery of a memory I cannot quite place. You carry three bags, all of them filled with strips of fabric. You have beautiful, soapy skin. When I see you, I think of the figure in Manet's picnic staring from the canvas at the viewer. You gaze out. Naked in the world, while the people around you fasten their jackets and converse with each other. You explain that you are looking for someone to share your name, who will offer a sense of self to cling to. Grainy oblongs of light pattern the floorboards from the streetlamp outside.

Day 67

Who knows if the day will get any brighter, feel any more like spring is near, a breeze lifting clothing, a sky filled with only blue. But I do know we kept our appointment, that there is eagerness in your voice and willingness to hear what I say, to listen to my advice. This fills me with a cloud of achievement, a white puff of pleasure in the satisfaction of helping someone, of ordinary life, and the sensation of possibility. Then comes the emotion of the last year so heavy: the wasted energy of words that never found their expression.

Day 68

Your jackets are loaded for the evening ahead. All three of you carry wine
bottles in your pockets; all three of you clutch packages of food, have
Millwall scarves around your neck. You laugh deeply, your pink mouth
opening slightly as you do, your moustache substantial on your lip. You
bare a hundred teeth, yellowing but not quite unclean. You like the cover
of my book, I tell you about the author, that she's a friend and she's written
about the Arctic. Stumbling into me, you grab the rail and not my book-
holding arm. We acknowledge this moment with relief.

Day 69

Years have passed and the words you say are not the words you mean but rather the words you read on the information panels in the museum you work in, on the script they gave you once. You tell me about foundlings, what it meant to be abandoned, be the abandoner, to house the abandoned. A mother was so poor that she could only offer a brazil nut shell as a farewell gift, a painter turned to religion, an artist lost her child, I am not the only person who can talk too much. These are things I learn today.

Day 70

I buy a packet of wasabi peas to clear my head. I chew on a handful as I select birthday biscuits. You treat me as a confidante, as though you are telling me great secrets about the use of butter on these ones, the double chocolate on that. You start to tell me about your diet and lift both hands to your chest in a gesture of both distress and vulnerability, which is so feminine and reliant on rescue, that I avert my eyes from such exposure of emotion. I choose quickly, you want more than I'm willing to give.

Day 71

You appear to me hazy because I am too ingrained in the dense earth of my life to be uprooted. When we speak, you frown and shrug, maybe not in that order, or maybe you didn't do that at all. You are bespectacled and prone to laugh. I, on the other hand, feel morose, with eyes inclined to spill. Last week, I tried to ask questions of someone I knew wouldn't answer and knew I knew that too. At the time, I thought this was meaningful but now I think that there are things I will never know about people.

Day 72

I remember oranges and you don't mind me leaving the queue momentarily to find some. When you say, Of course, you press my arm in sympathy and recognition. This may be the thing that breaks me today, that stops me in my tracks before driving me forward, turning a corner, making something work, letting everything happen. When I return, you are touching my yoghurts, reading the ingredients, as though you are making them yours, protecting them in my absence and amusing yourself with the cherry-ness of them. On days like this, I want to take my strangers home with me.

Day 73

Luckily, you come to the door so I can speak to a stranger without leaving my house. You hand me two parcels and I tell you there must be a mistake. The name, I don't recognise, the weight seems too significant. You convince me to hold onto the items, despite my reluctance. You are a man of many colours, your hat is green and pink, lips red. You wear blue and there is an icing sugar sprinkle of snow on your shoulders. This is a single exchange for you, but for me you're the only person I have seen today.

Day 74

This morning I learn that quinuituq is Inuit for deep patience, used to describe
the wait for a seal at a hole in the ice. The sleepy way the afternoon unfolds
pleases me. At the pub, I talk, greet, confide, spill and wrap birthday ribbon
in my hair. I order hummus and flatbread, you speak of African countries
and also Belgium. You think I'm the artists I work with. I try to explain, but
to distinguish myself makes less sense to us both. You ask if I have many
friends. You say, The world is made anew on Friday evenings.

Day 75

I walk to and from the station, carrying nothing but a sensation of calm, like a rucksack of cool, a handbag of relaxation. It is Saturday and I have been in good company. I see you, buying a croissant; a chewing bovine, you. Here, you are waiting watch-watching, then no longer alone. You are shouting on your telephone, such a pretty toy. I see you there, bitterness at your daughter. And you, fingers gripping fresh flowers, expression glazed. I speak to none of you today, but I rise up and watch. To these little things, I will always be open.

Day 76

With a pink balloon in one of your hands, a pile of chewed cakes and plates in the other, I ask you where you learned to dance. It's a moment from Fame, from Cabaret: your face lights up, it's the question you love to answer. All your life, since a girl, ballet classes, the ribbons, your grandmother, ballrooms, the foxtrot, the New York academy, Paris (once), and now a teacher by the sea. I tell you I think you dance beautifully because I know that, sweaty brow, tired feet, eyes smudged, this is what you will most like to hear.

Day 77

We're late but you are patient enough to smile us to our seats. If you had time, I'd ask you about what we missed so we could decide if our morning was lost for reason enough. I'd say that you are one of those people who are fine and a thinker, or generous and a good friend. In my memory, you are wearing a suit. I think you had a bow tie and held a photograph of your mother, but perhaps it wasn't of her. A woman in the front row swigs brandy and creases her programme between her palms.

Day 78

A woman jams her buggy into the right hand side of the escalator, trying to manoeuvre the lumbering bulk alongside a series of unyielding bodies. You smile at the child strapped in, opening and closing its fists. Hello, you say as you walk pass. Hello, hello, as you march down the steps. The air in the tube station is thick. You have a briefcase, swing it as you saunter. I'm behind you, direct you to a train. Then the baby comes by again and we say, Goodbye, goodbye. The mother is unaware, busy wheeling her child through streets of people.

Day 79

You're the nicest person I have met in a long time. You're as familiar as I am with speaking to strangers and you know just what to do. You are hunched in your shoulders, have tightly cropped hair. A gentle voice, a gentle manner. You and I are early for the meeting, but you were the one who walked mistakenly into the wrong room. You are like me, except male, thirty years older, more eager. I can tell you're a writer and one of the good ones. Your mind ticks, a clock of academic knowledge. I bring you strong coffee.

Day 80

Your only power these days is to escape into your own body. It starts with averting your eyes, sending your thoughts to your toes, letting your hair fall over your face. It gives you a sense of being in control. Whilst your children grow tall, you are watchful and careful to laugh when things are funny and flatten your mouth in sympathy when they aren't. Maybe you had a friend called Rose who was the daring one, who rolled her socks to her ankles and tore the pins from her hair. You scan my items, but you're not really here.

Day 81

You like my dress and start groping the material with your big hands. It's a miniscule toilet area. I'm not sure where to look. Your friend joins us in the queue and she's fond of the dress too. I've always wanted to make clothes, she says, as we marvel at the material. Two people exit the cubicle wiping noses, looking like twenty year olds, acting like toddlers. We all examine our eyelashes. You discover you no longer need to stay here. I see you later, a fur draped over your shoulders, shouting abuse at a police officer in the street.

Day 82

This is not a city for you. You stare straight ahead as I ask you about the journey. Will it be long or short? Will I reach the tube station in time? And, what is it about north-west London that makes me feel so incensed? The vortex of suburban life, the space filled with brick housing, neat gardens, guarded expressions, girls in mittens and baby Uggs. Your face is blank, closed and checked, directionless. You're looking into the air, the windscreen marking no boundary for your eyes. You stop the bus, start again, press a single button, drive once more.

Day 83

A helicopter is circling in a weight of clouds. It lingers in the grainy sky. We scramble across a river, slip on the sodden soil. Then the heath opens up and it's Kenwood House: vivid white, grass green, sky creamy blue grey. You stride through the gates, tell us we must leave and give directions. Your wellied feet are dry and you're wearing a National Trust sweatshirt. My feet sink into the mud. This is because Primark do not offer a waterproof option and I rarely think ahead. You are brisk and it's starting to rain. And yet, and yet.

Day 84

I am in a rush. I hear the sound of my footsteps, the wheezing of the automatic
door opening, the selection of a basket, the apology from a small child and
then the crinkle of packets. At the checkout, you have a yoghurt and a bottle
of water and tell me you don't like to eat. This information invites discussion.
I am tempted to comment on your hipbones and the strain of your cheeks
but I smile instead, tell you I adore the taste of hot tea, creamy scones with
jam. I watch you count out £1.39 in small change.

Day 85

It's fashion week and it's right now. On the door you stand, poised clipboard, broad smile and chipped teeth. I tell you how beautiful I think Liberty is, the fouth floor regally looking down with a timber gaze. I could also tell you what I know about this department store: made from the wood of two ships, bombed for its Rushdie books once, tiers that look into a central interior courtyard. However, none of this is vaguely or voguely interesting. There are nude photographs to see, wine to sip, women with elongated limbs, anguished eyes and puffed fringes to sidestep.

Day 86

Umbrellas become weapons as we fight to the tube station. You elbow me as you pass and I square up, ready to fight. You say, What? I say, What? and we stare and we pause and you flick water in my eyes. I take each of my gloves, roll them together into a ball and aim at your nose. You see my arm draw back, raise an eyebrow and kick me in the knees. Today was going to be a fine day, a light day. As I lay on the ground, many people avoid me, many people try to help.

Day 87

I'm walking in circles and you ask me if I find it hard to make a decision. I tell you I will answer you later. I have seen every shoulder bag on this street, I've asked a stranger where she purchased hers. You wait by the door, ready to snatch at shoplifters or to grab conversation. From my eyelashes, a drop of rain hesitates then falls. The tear of water slips down my face and I say I never can find the answers. Sunshine on a grey day can be so strange and sad. I don't manage today so well.

Day 88

I ask you a detailed question and your answer is simply No. I laugh hard and
try again. This time it's Yes. You have a gap between your teeth, a belly that
rests on the counter. I type in my pin code and you make enquiries about
my afternoon. You speak in haiku so I respond in kind. Train northbound
waiting, delayed inevitably - by wind or else rain. We try again. I squeeze in
a long word where a short would do. I take my ticket. It is finally Friday and
I am thinking of words, or else sleep.

Day 89

The Greek restaurant just out of London – it is here I must speak to a stranger. This room is full of excited girls with curled hair and brave, stiff dresses. They sidestep on the dancefloor, clap clap, eyes wild and frightened. I ask you about the bill and you look to me hatefully, angry for my asking. You have thick fingers, a small nose and a hollow mouth. You won't look at the customers who are shrieking at the Michael Jackson impersonator behind us. You are so very gloomy but, at their lot, some must despair for others to celebrate.

Day 90

Your fingers grip the edges of the staircase where we stand. I nod reassuringly to you, and your look is relief or even reprieve. She's playing a sonata, your daughter, and she's nervous. A freckled and tiny person, just a schoolgirl uncomfortable in oversized casual clothes, out of uniform. The music is soothing, clear, light, the room quiet just for her and the piano. She finishes and you applaud and you wave, and your daughter stands, looks out into the audience and raises her hand to a sturdy woman in the second row. It's the wrong mother but close enough.

Day 91

We have a conversation about our values. How do we feel about them, about each other? If we had morals, what would they be? We have three full hours to decide and then what? Then we know. You come in late and I ask you which side you are on. You have delicate lips and when you speak, the truth comes out. Out it comes, from your mouth to my ears. It journeys easily; it's done so before. You pick words from a low orchard of trees you have nearby. And only the ripest, most apposite ones you will taste.

Day 92

You hand me an envelope with a cheque I can't accept. For such a public transaction, we show no awkwardness. Life, which can seem so effortless and repetitive, is really a marvellously complex sequence of exchanges with people you know and can reassure you, and those who are strangers and cannot. You are so interested in me, and the way I articulate my thoughts. I use flamboyant hand gestures, suck on my glass of juice, tell you my ideas on transformation. We think life carries on elsewhere but where we are, right here, is the very centre of the universe.

Day 93

You serve me with a smile. You really like me. I have fennel tea. For you, every customer has to be reckoned with. There's solitude at home and then there's company at work. You're bewildered by my choice. Do I want milk? I don't. Do I want tap water? Yes. You want me to stay and talk. You raise your hand and I'm a puppy to your instruction. Stay, stay. I wait and count your tips. Coppers and some silver. My drinks are here. You ask me with your eyes, Why not stay? Have a heart. Why not just stay?

Day 94

You tell me it won't hurt a bit. I perch on the examination table and roll up my sleeve. Tapping at my veins, you inadvertently drop everything on the floor. Scuffling near my feet, you pick up spare needles and containers while one hand keeps the point in my arm throughout. You ask me if I'll return to work. I will, but not before I eat a pain au chocolate and gape at the blue sky. As I leave I think, don't speak to me: if you wish me luck, I'll take your words and throw them out the window.

Day 95

It's Camden you need to get off at, I say to you when you ask. Your girlfriend is drunk and gazing blankly around the carriage. I like her for her aquamarine eyeliner and sun-bleached hair. You ask me questions and say you're from Sydney. She is stressed, briefly, because you're late. I assure you that you'll be fine for time, though I have no idea where you are heading. When we step off the tube, the ambition of your aim is infectious. I also speed towards the next train, desperate to meet my deadline of no time and doesn't matter.

Day 96

Floor plans cover the walls, ceiling and sofa. Standing against an open window, you're shivering yet pleased: all in the name of art. This 1960s housing estate is condemned, though you don't know why. This building will be replaced, but you're not sure what with. This building offers free furniture after 10pm; however you can't be certain. I take your responses to mean that site-specific creativity in urban spaces does not automatically bestow knowledge of the place. You wear several scarves and hold a walkie-talkie. I try again: You must be cold. You cheer up: Right, right yes I am.

Day 97

I allow myself a little rudeness. You tell me about an event you've just seen and I look down at you – you're small – and say, What? Then louder, WHAT? A writer, you inform me, and very good. I let my mouth open. A yawn? I think it is. Someone pushes past me. I swear at them, or at least mouth the words. Your wife praises the speaker she heard. She's tall, hunches to hear us. I say, Uh instead of Pardon and roll my eyes. When we say goodbye, I am nice again. A real pleasure to meet you both.

Day 98

A stranger as a challenge. You are on the telephone but I need to communicate with you. A gesture, then. You ignore me. A wave. Can I pass, please? You avert your eyes. I lean over you to order my cheese salad sandwich. I hear the tinny voice from your handset. Someone is crying. What I say is this: Don't go. Or do go. Stay with him, or don't. Eat well, or not. Settle in this country, or don't. Be ridiculous, but sometimes don't be. The only place from which you don't have to return is the journey to yourself.

Day 99

My thoughts leap from here to there. Happily, for relief, there are gossip magazines. I watch as you select an armful of brightly coloured publications telling you all that's necessary about Cheryl, Jordan and Jennifer. I flick through one and say aloud, Sex Text Saga. You reply, Excuse me, reaching for one more. I scoff but here I am admiring the free shampoo offer with Glamour. I ask you about Tess and Vernon. And then real life walks in through the double doors and says, now then you two. There it is asking, Who is right and who is wrong?

Day 100

Tonight, I think of my younger self with eyes of endurance and focus, eyes wide and credulous. You take a handmade scroll and draw it open. For you, this evening is veiled in a fog of revelries. You tug at the gold ribbon, unwrap the printed paper. You're reading and I'm by your side marvelling at my own work. I lose my cool though I probably never had it, or felt it once and took it, held it, watched it vanish again. What I don't have within me by this age, I choose to lack. And you're the final stranger.